NO ANIMALS, NO PLANTS

SPECIES AT RISK

Library of Congress Cataloging-in-Publication Data

Irvine, Sarah.
 No animals, no plants : species at risk / by Sarah Irvine.
     p. cm. -- (Shockwave)
 Includes index.
 ISBN-10: 0-531-17766-1 (lib. bdg.)
 ISBN-13: 978-0-531-17766-2 (lib. bdg.)
 ISBN-10: 0-531-15496-3 (pbk.)
 ISBN-13: 978-0-531-15496-0 (pbk.)
 1. Endangered species--North America--Juvenile literature. 2. Endangered plants--
North America--Juvenile literature. I. Title. II. Series.

  QL83.I79 2007
  578.68--dc22

2007016312

Published in 2008 by Children's Press, an imprint of Scholastic Inc.,
557 Broadway, New York, New York 10012
www.scholastic.com

SCHOLASTIC, CHILDREN'S PRESS, and associated logos are trademarks
and/or registered trademarks of Scholastic Inc.

08 09 10 11 12 13 14 15 16 17
10 9 8 7 6 5 4 3 2 1

Printed in China through Colorcraft Ltd., Hong Kong

Author: Sarah Irvine
Educational Consultant: Ian Morrison
Editor: Mary Atkinson
Designer: Amy Lam
Photo Researcher: Jamshed Mistry

Photographs by: Big Stock Photo (tree, coral, p. 9; fox glove, p. 11); **Brand X** (turtle, p. 9); **Digital Vision** (p. 14; p. 16; leopard, p. 19); **Dynamic Graphics** (p. 3); **Getty Images** (jaguar, p. 19; park bus, p. 23; p. 26; Robert Bakewell, p. 28; tiger, pp. 32–33); **Ingram Image Library** (walrus, panda, rhino, p. 8; tiger, chameleon, dolphin, eagle, frog, p. 9); **Image State** (p. 10); **Jennifer and Brian Lupton** (teenagers, pp. 32–33); **More Images/NPL** (shark, dodo, pp. 18–19); **Photolibrary** (moth, p. 18; p. 24; wolf, p. 25; corn cobs, p. 27; foal, p. 28; clean-up volunteers, p. 31); **Stock.Xchng** (flower, p. 9); **TopFoto/www.stockcentral.co.nz** (volunteer planting, p. 23); **Tranz/Corbis** (cover; p. 7; p. 11; pp. 12–13; p. 15; p. 17; pp. 20–22; fox, p. 25; date palm, p. 27; pp. 29–30; girl recycling, p. 31)

All illustrations and other photographs © Weldon Owen Education Inc.

SHOCKWAVE
SCIENCE

NO ANIMALS, NO PLANTS

SPECIES AT RISK

Sarah Irvine

children's press®

An imprint of Scholastic Inc.

NEW YORK • TORONTO • LONDON • AUCKLAND • SYDNEY
MEXICO CITY • NEW DELHI • HONG KONG
DANBURY, CONNECTICUT

CHECK THESE OUT!

SHOCKER

Stuff to Shock,
Surprise, and
Amaze You

Quick Recaps
and Notable
Notes

Word Stunners
and Other Oddities

The Heads-Up
on Expert Reading

Links to More
Information

CONTENTS

biodiversity (*bye oh duh VUR suh tee*) the variety of different species living in an area

conservationist a person who works to protect wild plants and animals and their environments

ecosystem (*EE koh siss tuhm*) a community of animals and plants interacting with their environment

endangered close to becoming extinct

extinct (*ek STINGKT*) no longer existing

habitat an area where a plant or an animal lives naturally

species (*SPEE sheez*) a group of plants or animals that share common characteristics and are able to reproduce

. . . .

For additional vocabulary, see Glossary on page 34.

The *bio-* beginning in words such as *biodiversity* refers to "life and living things." Related words include:
biology – the study of living things
biosphere – the part of the world where life exists
biodegradable – able to be broken down by living things

A **conservationist** prunes young trees for forestry conservation.

Nobody knows exactly how many plants and animals live on the earth. So far, scientists have counted about 260,000 different **species** of plants. They have also counted about 1,500,000 different species of animals. New species are being found all the time. Many of them are tiny, one-celled creatures. Others are insects found only in tall jungle trees or other places scientists have trouble reaching. However, the actual number of species on the earth is going down. Many plants and animals are becoming **extinct**. Some become extinct before we even discover them. This is mainly because of the things humans are doing. It is up to us to learn about why this happens and to help stop it.

What's the Problem?

Why should we protect other species? Some people think that we have an **obligation** to do so. They believe all animals and plants have a right to exist. Others think that each species is important in its own way. Without many of the species alive today, the world would simply be much less interesting. Imagine, for example, that the only way to see lions or elephants was in old photographs and movies. If we do not act now to protect those animals, that could be the case 50 years from now.

The cheetah is an animal ▶ in trouble. There are fewer than 15,000 left. They do not breed well in zoos. Once they become extinct in the wild, they will probably soon become extinct altogether.

Another important reason for protecting species is that each one is **unique**. We still do not know a lot about many species. We do know that some plant species produce chemicals that cure diseases. Scientists are working with communities around the world to find out what they know about the healing properties of local plants. It takes a long time to test each plant to see how it can benefit us. Many plants may be gone before we can test them. The earth's rain forests are an important source of many medicinal plants. However, these forests are being destroyed, and the people who live in them are moving to cities. Both the source of the plants and the source of knowledge about them could soon be lost.

▲ The foxglove is a poisonous plant. However, a drug that is made from it is used to treat heart disease. In the 1700s, William Withering, an English doctor, noticed a herbalist was using it to treat patients. He investigated further and discovered its benefits.

◀ This rain-forest dweller is skilled at climbing tall trees to collect medicinal plants. He knows which trees to climb. He also knows at what times of year he will find the plant parts he needs.

Does it really matter if some species become extinct? Why should we save dangerous sharks or biting insects? Each species is part of an **ecosystem**. Ecosystems have a natural balance. When one thing is changed, the whole system is affected. For example, in the mid-1900s, many people used DDT, a newly developed **pesticide**, to kill insect pests. However, DDT killed useful insects, as well as harmful ones. Birds that ate the insects laid weak eggs, which often crushed before they hatched. The birds that did hatch had trouble finding enough insects to eat. Soon there were fewer birds in the countryside. DDT was banned in the U.S. and many other countries in the 1970s. Since then, many of the damaged ecosystems have begun to recover.

Even the killing of **predators** can cause problems. For example, if all the foxes in a field were killed, the population of rabbits might grow very large. They might then eat too many plants, killing off important plant species. Without their food, the rabbits too could die out.

Birds spread the seeds of many ▶ plants by eating them. As they fly, they deposit the seeds in their droppings. Without birds, even the plants would suffer.

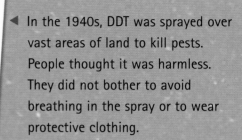

◀ In the 1940s, DDT was sprayed over vast areas of land to kill pests. People thought it was harmless. They did not bother to avoid breathing in the spray or to wear protective clothing.

A Woodland Food Web

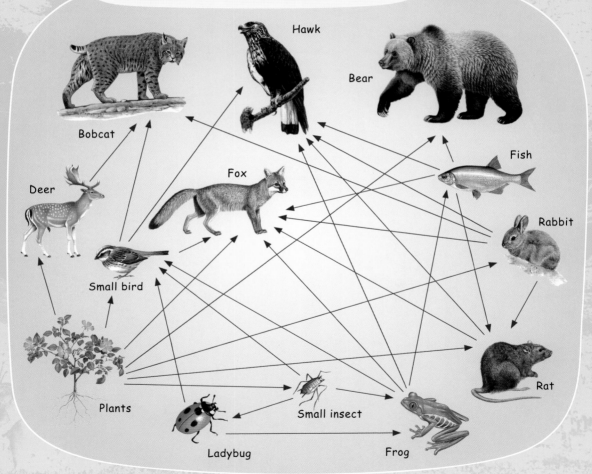

Hawk

Bear

Bobcat

Fish

Deer

Fox

Rabbit

Small bird

Rat

Plants

Small insect

Ladybug

Frog

▲ A food web is type of a diagram. It shows us how some species in an ecosystem depend on each other. Each arrow goes from a species to an animal that eats it.

Why Are Species Endangered?

There are four main reasons why species get into trouble. The most important one right now is **habitat** destruction. As the human population grows, people use more and more land. Forests are cut down for timber or to clear land. Grasslands are planted with crops. Wetlands are drained to provide more land. Each time this happens, there is slightly less land available for wild animals and plants.

The first sentence indicates what the next chunk of text will be about. It sure makes reading easier when you have a good idea of what to expect.

Habitat destruction can prevent large animals from finding enough food or a mate. In China, people are planting bamboo "roads" so that pandas can move from one pocket of bamboo forest to the next.

Another problem is overhunting. In the last few centuries, people have developed more effective hunting equipment. Guns have replaced spears. Enormous nets have replaced smaller, handmade fishing nets. It has become easier to kill animals in large numbers. Some animals, such as tigers and seals, have been shot because people thought they would harm their own **livestock** or catches of fish. Millions of dolphins have died after getting caught in the huge nets used to catch tuna.

▲ In Africa, some animals are having trouble finding food because of the number of tourists. A lion cannot sneak up on its prey when vehicles full of excited people keep following it.

Many animals are **endangered** because people hunt them. Elephants are hunted for their ivory. Whales are hunted for their meat. Other animals, such as rare parrots, are caught alive to sell as pets. The people who hunt or **poach** these animals do so to make money. If more people around the world became aware of the problem and stopped buying these products, the trade in rare species would stop.

There is a fourth major reason why animals and plants are in trouble. It is because they have to compete with new species brought into their environment by people. As people have moved around the world, they have taken plants, farm animals, pets, and pests with them. Hardy new plants have taken over land where rare, native plants once grew. Animals such as rats have often brought diseases. Some have eaten local lizards, birds, and birds' eggs. They have also competed with local animals for food.

▼ These customs officers are inspecting a haul of elephants' ivory that they confiscated.

Four Reasons Why Species Are in Trouble

- habitat destruction
- overhunting
- trade in rare species
- competition from introduced species

◀ In Southeast Asia, adult orangutans are being killed so that the babies can be sold as pets. If more people were aware of this, the market for baby orangutans could be reduced. Without that public awareness, the future of the species is in doubt.

Many birds in New Zealand ▶ are flightless. When Europeans migrated to the country in the 1800s, they brought cats and dogs with them. Today, rare birds such as the kiwi are in trouble. This is partly because they are hunted by animals such as dogs and cannot fly away to escape them.

◀ In the 1800s, sailors released goats on the Galápagos Islands. The sailors wanted a supply of goats for food. However, the goats ate the plants eaten by rare giant tortoises. The tortoises nearly became extinct. Now the goats have been removed. The number of tortoises is slowly increasing.

17

The Red List

How do we know which species are endangered? Many conservation groups publish information about the animals they are concerned with. However, there is one organization that attempts to get a global picture of all threatened plants and animals. This is the IUCN, or the International Union for Conservation of Nature and Natural Resources. The IUCN publishes the IUCN Red List of Threatened Species. The list gives the conservation status of as many plants and animals as the IUCN has been able to determine are threatened. So far, the Red List includes more than 41,000 species, including 12,000 plant species.

The IUCN is not large enough to collect all the data itself. Instead, other organizations around the world help out. The Red List is published on the Internet so that as many people as possible can access it.

IUCN is an abbreviation, or short form. It is not pronounced like a word: each letter is spoken separately, like *PC* for "personal computer," or *DIY* for "do it yourself." Abbreviations where the entire word is pronounced, such as *NASA* or *UNICEF*, are called acronyms.

Spanish moon moth

SHOCKER

According to the IUCN, 40 percent of all species are threatened. This includes 23 percent of mammals, 52 percent of insects, and 100 percent of lichens.

The IUCN Categories

Each species on the Red List is in a category. The species in the critically endangered, endangered, and vulnerable categories are described as being threatened. Data deficient species are ones that are probably threatened but there is not enough evidence to prove it.

Category		Example	
		Animal	Plant
EX	Extinct	Dodo bird	St. Helena olive
EW	Extinct in the wild	Socorro dove	Wood's cycad
CR	Critically endangered	Hawksbill turtle	Wollemi pine
EN	Endangered	Giant panda	Ginkgo tree
VU	Vulnerable	Great white shark	Venus flytrap
NT	Near threatened	Jaguar	Christmas cactus
LC	Least concern	Mallard duck	Cobra lily
DD	Data deficient	Spanish moon moth	Robust oak

Jaguar

Venus flytrap

Dodo bird

Great white shark

19

The Endangered Species Act

In 1973, the U.S. government passed the Endangered Species Act, or ESA. This law is intended to save plants and animals in trouble in the United States. The ESA has a list of U.S. species in trouble. Once a species is on the list, it gets protection. A recovery plan is put in place. Laws prevent people from hunting, collecting, or harming it in other ways. The species' habitat is also protected, because it could not survive if its habitat were damaged.

▲ The San Francisco garter snake is endangered.

Two organizations are in charge of this work. They are the FWS (U.S. Fish and Wildlife Service) and NOAA (National Oceanic and Atmospheric Administration). These organizations can decide to place a species on the list. A person or outside organization can also ask for a species to be placed on the list. First they need to compile a **petition** to show that other people are also concerned about that species.

▲ The northern Idaho ground squirrel is on the ESA list as threatened. It is found only in a 20-square-mile area of Idaho. Fewer than 500 are thought to exist.

The ESA Categories

The ESA list categorizes animals in a different way from the IUCN. In the ESA system, "threatened" is a category in its own right. Animals in the endangered group get greater protection than those in the threatened group.

Category		Example	
		Animal	Plant
EX	Extinct	Wooly mammoth	*Kokia lanceolata*
E	Endangered	Gray bat	Key tree cactus
T	Threatened	Bald eagle	Gowen cypress
CS	Candidate species	Yellow-billed cuckoo	Basalt daisy

▲ Candidate species, such as the yellow-billed cuckoo, are endangered or threatened species that are not on the ESA list. This is because other species are considered higher priority.

SHOCKER

The polar bear and the gray wolf are both being considered for ESA listing. The polar bear is thought to be threatened. The gray wolf is thought to be endangered.

The salt marsh bird's-beak ▶ is an endangered plant found in California and Mexico. **Conservationists** regularly count and measure the plant at the Sweetwater Marsh National Wildlife Refuge near San Diego.

Parks, Reserves, and Gardens

One way people are working to help save plants and animals is by creating national parks and reserves. In these places, land is set aside to remain natural. Different countries and different reserves have different regulations. Sometimes all people are banned from living there. Often hunting is banned or restricted. Park rangers patrol parks and reserves to ensure people stick to the regulations. However, in places where people are poor, there is pressure on governments to allow people to live, farm, or hunt in parks and reserves.

At the other end of the scale, some people are creating their own mini-reserves. They are working to ensure that their own garden or neighborhood park is full of trees and other plants. Small patches of green in towns and cities can provide homes for many creatures, as well as restful places for people to meet or relax.

When I read "At the other end of the scale ...," I wasn't sure what the author meant. Fish scales? Weighing scales? As I continued to read, it became obvious that this was the type of scale that compares things.

▲ In Utah's Zion National Park, propane-powered buses transport tourists around the park. The buses are quiet and environmentally friendly. This is thought to save 4,000 vehicle trips each day.

◀ Every year, millions of people visit National Parks in the United States. This group of tourists have stopped their cars to observe wildlife in Yellowstone National Park.

▲ Often there is not enough money in park and reserve budgets. Many parks are run with donated money and with the help of **volunteers**.

Variety Is Important

When people talk about **biodiversity**, they are talking about the variety of plants and animals in an area. Conservationists work at different levels to protect the biodiversity in an ecosystem.

- Conservationists want to keep alive a large population of each species. This is called **genetic** diversity. It means that if there is a change, such as global warming, at least some individuals might survive and breed. The species will not become extinct.

- Conservationists want most of the native species in an ecosystem to remain living there. This is called species diversity. Sometimes if a species is lost from an ecosystem, conservationists will **reintroduce** it from elsewhere.

- Conservationists want to save as many ecosystems as possible. This is called ecosystem diversity. Each ecosystem is unique. The plants and animals that live naturally in Oregon are different from those in Virginia. There may be thousands of species in a single ecosystem.

▲ In 1994, the ivory-billed woodpecker was declared extinct. Then, in 2004, a bird was spotted in a wildlife refuge in Arkansas. Conservationists say that its possible survival may be due to the work of many people to protect its habitat.

Concerned with plants and animals

Work to keep species alive

Conservationists

Work for species diversity

Work for ecosystem diversity

In Yellowstone National Park, all the wolves died out. The elk population grew very large. The elk fed on plants that other animals depend on. Then, in 1995, a wolf population was reintroduced from Canada. The wolves keep the elk population under control. This allows more plants to grow. The plants again provide homes and food for animals such as birds and beavers.

The tiny Santa Cruz Island fox lives ▶ only on a small island off the coast of California. It was nearly wiped out in the 1990s by golden eagles moving to the island. Conservationists relocated the golden eagles. Then they reintroduced bald eagles, which used to live there before they were killed off with DDT. Bald eagles do not eat foxes.

Plants and Crops

Endangered plants need our protection as much as endangered animals do. They provide homes and food for living things. They are an important part of many ecosystems. Some rare plants may hold the key to new life-saving medicines, fuels, healthful foods, and other things needed by people.

Many of the seeds sold to farmers are bred to produce fruits and vegetables that are large or **disease-resistant**. The problem is that the crops often do not produce **viable** seeds that can grow into new plants. This means that farmers are forced to buy new seeds from the seed companies each year.

Many plants reproduce by producing seeds. Some seeds can lie **dormant** for years at a time. Then, when the conditions are right, they **germinate** and grow into new plants. The ability of seeds to lie dormant allows plants to survive droughts and other hard times. Some organizations store seeds from rare plants so that they can be planted if all the living plants of a species die out.

Modern date palm

▲ The oldest-known seed to grow into a new plant was 2,000 years old. It was a Judean date palm seed found at the site of an ancient fortress in Israel. It was planted in 2005. Research scientist Sarah Sallon wants to test the plant to see if it has any medicinal qualities that modern date palms do not have.

SHOCKER

In Norway, a seed bank is planned that will be able to survive nuclear war or severe storms. It will be built in a tunnel below frozen ground. It will have thick, concrete walls, air locks, and bombproof doors.

The *-ate* at the end of a word such as *germinate* often indicates that it is a verb. The noun form often ends with *-ion*, for example: *germinate – germination; cultivate – cultivation; pollinate – pollination.*

◄ Heirloom plants are old varieties of plants that produce viable seeds. Some people plant them to ensure plant biodiversity. Others think the fruit or vegetables they produce are tastier and healthier.

27

Genes and Genetics

Every species of plant or animal has its own kind of **DNA**. This determines what the species will look like, how it will get food, how big it will grow, and so on. Early humans learned that if they planted seeds from plants that produced big crops, they were likely to get more plants with big crops. They started selecting plants for the qualities they wanted. Over time, this process has changed the DNA of many species.

◄ Scientists have now learned how to **clone** animals. The foal on the right is a clone of its mother, which stands beside it. However, many people think that this is **unethical**, especially if someone were to clone a person.

In the late 1700s, Englishman Robert Bakewell made a science of breeding better livestock. He bred much fatter sheep. Before that, most sheep were raised mainly for their wool.

More recently, scientists have learned how to change the DNA of plant and animal species in a **laboratory**. This is called genetic modification. They attempt to produce species that grow faster, yield bigger crops, or are pest- and disease-resistant. Some people believe that genetic modification will provide more food for more people. However, other people argue that this could upset the balance of ecosystems or cause other unknown problems. These people insist that there would be enough food for everyone if it were distributed fairly.

Now that's interesting! I know a little about DNA from science programs on TV. But I thought it was just something to do with people. I never realized that animals and plants have DNA too.

▼ Genetically modified plants are grown in selected fields and greenhouses. There they are tested to be sure that they are safe. Some people argue that this does not show what will happen if these plants are introduced into other ecosystems.

The Future

The only thing we know for sure about the future for plants and animals is that it will be different from today. This is partly because ecosystems are constantly changing. The earth's weather systems change and affect living things. We know, for example, that the Sahara desert in Africa was once **savanna**. It was home to animals such as giraffes and hippos. Now, the Sahara is spreading and parts of Africa are becoming dryer.

Natural disasters, such as floods and meteorite strikes, can also change an environment. Some scientists think that it was a meteorite strike that led to the extinction of the dinosaurs. However, what people do now will probably affect plants and animals more than anything else.

If we work to save endangered species, the world will be the richer for it. Each species that is helped will make a difference. It is up to each one of us to find out about the species at risk in our area. If we don't do anything to help directly, at least we can try to cause no further harm.

◀ These rock paintings are between 2,000 and 4,000 years old. They are in the middle of the Sahara desert. They show us that hippos lived in that area in the past.

Cause	Effect
• weather systems change	• savannas can become deserts
• natural disasters	• extinction of species
• working together to save species	• makes the world a richer place

▲ Today many more people are taking better care of the environment. These volunteers helped clean up a riverbank in Detroit, Michigan.

What Can You Do?

✓ Find out what plants and animals are at risk near you. Teach other people about these species, so that the people will not harm them.

✓ Do not litter. Litter is harmful to animals.

✓ Recycle as much plastic, paper, glass, and metal as you can. That way there will be less waste in landfills.

✓ Ask your family or class to join a conservation group. You could even take part in events such as tree-planting days.

✓ Subscribe to a magazine about animals.

✓ If you have a backyard, find out what you can do to attract local birds, butterflies, and other creatures to it.

31

...the past, zoo animals often lived in small, bare cages. Many animals were rare species taken from their natural environments without thought to how the species would survive. Zoos today are often wildlife conservation parks. They are places where animals are provided with large enclosures that are as close to their natural habitat as possible.

WHAT DO YOU THINK?

Do you think it is fair to keep animals in zoos, or should all zoo animals be returned to the wild?

PRO

I think we need zoos. If some species were returned, they would be hunted to extinction. Other species no longer have anywhere to go. Also, zoos are a good way to educate people. When people know about wild animals, they are more likely to want to protect them.

Tiger at Melbourne Zoo, Australia

Zoos are also places where animals that are endangered or extinct in the wild can live and breed. This has enabled some species to survive. They are also places where people can go to see and learn about wild animals.

CON

I think zoos are cruel. It is not fair to make animals live in a small area and be stared at by crowds of people. Wherever possible, I think we should restore animals' natural environments. People living nearby should be hired to guard against poachers. Then we should return the animals to the places where they came from.

GLOSSARY

clone (*KLOHN*) to reproduce a plant or an animal so that it is identical to its parent

disease-resistant able to fight off diseases

DNA the molecules in every cell of an organism that carry the genetic code, which determines characteristics of that organism, such as eye color

dormant in an inactive state; alive but not moving, growing, or feeding

genetic to do with genes, which are portions of DNA that code for specific characteristics, such as hair color

germinate to start growing into a new plant

laboratory a room where scientists perform experiments and study their results

livestock animals raised on a farm

obligation something that it is one's duty to do

pesticide a chemical that kills pests

petition a list of signatures of people who all agree on something they want to change

poach to kill or capture animals illegally

predator an animal that hunts and eats other animals

reintroduce to bring a plant or an animal species back into an area where it once lived

savanna (*suh VAN uh*) a flat grass plain with few trees, found in tropical areas

unethical not ethical; not right or correct; wrong

unique (*yoo NEEK*) different from everything else

viable (*VYE uh buhl*) able to reproduce

volunteer a person who does work for no pay

Predator

FIND OUT MORE

BOOKS

Burnie, David. *Endangered Planet*. Kingfisher, 2004.

Cefrey, Holly. *Cloning and Genetic Engineering*. Scholastic Library Publishing, 2002.

Gunzi, Christiane. *The Best Book of Endangered and Extinct Animals*. Kingfisher, 2004.

Pollock, Steve. *Ecology*. DK Eyewitness Books, 2005.

Souza, D M. *Endangered Plants*. Franklin Watts, 2003.

WEB SITES

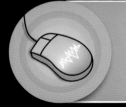

Go to the Web sites below to learn more about endangered species.

www.fws.gov/endangered/kids

www.worldwildlife.org/endangered

www.nps.gov/learn

www.kidsplanet.org/factsheets/map.html

www.iucn.org/themes/ssc/redlists/background_EN.htm

INDEX

ABOUT THE AUTHOR

Sarah Irvine enjoys researching and exploring our amazing planet and the plants and animals we share it with. She likes writing nonfiction books and sharing with young readers the information she discovers. Sarah believes that knowledge and understanding are the keys to taking care of our earth. "By understanding how the earth works and how plants and animals live, people can protect our precious planet."